Columbine

The Story of a Terrible American Tragedy

Jeff D. Lewis

Table of Contents

Introduction to Eric Harris and Dylan Klebold

Eric Harris's Childhood

Dylan Klebold's Childhood

April 20, 1999

The Aftermath

Columbine in The Movies

Speculation Continues

Introduction to Eric Harris and Dylan Klebold

It was April 20, 1999, when Eric Harris and Dylan Klebold grasped the nation's attention. Just the day before, the two boys were nothing more than the average American teenagers who were getting ready to graduate in only two weeks, or so they would have everyone believe.

For over a year, the two teenagers had been plotting to attack Columbine where they attended school, taking revenge on all of the people in it.

April 20, 1999, is a day that will forever be etched in the minds of those that were in school at the time, a day when innocence was lost and the world changed.

At the time of the shooting, Eric Harris was taking Luvox, which is an antidepressant. While Dylan Klebold's records remain sealed, one witness stated that he was taking Paxil as well as Zoloft, which are also antidepressants.

All three of these drugs are SSRIs also known as selective serotonin reuptake inhibitors and in 2004 the FDA issued a Public Health Advisory which stated that these medications could result in hostility, irritability, restlessness, insomnia, panic attacks, agitation, mania, as well as many other side effects.

Luvox, as well as Paxil, were listed on the top 10 list of prescription drugs which induced violence.

According to Dr. Ann Blake Tracy, who is the executive director of the International Coalition for Drug Awareness as well as the author of the book Prozac: Panacea or Pandora? the boy's brains were overloaded with serotonin which causes aggression and violent outbursts.

Eric had become obsessed with suicidal and homicidal thoughts within a few weeks after he began taking the prescription Zoloft but because of this obsession, he was then switched to Luvox which according to his autopsy was in his system when the shooting occurred.

Many people have tried to understand exactly what caused these boys to attack the school and their peers, however, they do not believe that any of the reasons make sense. It is these that believe the effects of the pharmaceuticals on children should be looked into further.

When you look at Dylan's journal, you can quickly tell that this is a boy that felt left out. There are pictures that depict him being far away from everyone else. He speaks of worrying about a boy in gym class, what he would do to Dylan, and states that his existence is s***.

Dylan stated that he feels he is going to eternally suffer, but that he thinks this reality is artificial.

On the next page, Dylan questions why another boy is being an A**hole, stating that the boy took 45 dollars from him as well as his knife and Zippo lighter. He states that he did get the lighter and knife back.

He goes on to state that he hates his life and he really wants to die right then. He writes that he has 11 antidepressants in his right hand and then goes on to say how the boy that is bullying his is lucky, that the boy has no idea how much he is suffering.

Later on in his journal, Dylan states that he is God compared to some of the brainless zombies.

On the last page of the journal, Dylan wrote out a list of things that he needed to do before he attacked the school. On the page is a drawing of him carrying guns, clips, knives, bullets, and poison.

On the first page of Eric Harris' journal, you find a list of the class of '98 and under it is written: "Top of the Should Have Died List."

Then from 4-10-1998 until 4-3-1999, you find:

Eric starts out by talking about how he hates the world, and about having self-awareness.

In the next entry, he continues to talk about self-awareness but states that he knows how to make all of them mad and how to make them feel bad. He also states that he is tired of parents, cops, teachers and God telling him what to do and what to say, that when they try to control him, it makes him not want to do it.

Eric states that he feels like God, that he believes everyone is lower than him.

Later, after getting his yearbook, Eric states that the human race is only good for killing and that the Earth should be given back to the animals.

Throughout the journal, you can see that Eric has an inflated sense of self-worth and that he thinks very poorly of other people.

It is October 22, 1998, when Eric first mentions the plan of attacking the school. He writes that he cannot be sidetracked by his sympathy or by mercy. Then he states that he is going to convince himself that everyone is nothing more than monsters from the video game 'Doom'.

It is November of that year that Eric talks about wanting guns but is having a hard time getting them. He states that at the time he has enough explosives to kill 100 people, but that it just is not enough.

November 22nd, Eric states that he was able to purchase the guns. He says that he has a carbine, shotgun, ammo, and a knife in the trunk of his car and that he had a lot of fun at the gun show he went to that day.

He also states that he is motivated, that this is his goal, that he is armed, and that the shooting is what he wants to do with his life.

On December 20th, 1998 Eric writes that he finds it funny that the KMFDM's new album entitled Adios would be released in April.

In the last entry, months have gone by since he wrote in his journal. Eric states that it is the first Friday night in the final month. He is focused on killing and states that he feels like he is in a movie at times.

Eric finishes by saying that he hates the people for leaving him out of so many fun things, that the weird Eric kid was not allowed to go along.

Just 17 days later, Eric would walk into his high school and open fire.

When you read the journals of Eric Harris and Dylan Klebold, you cannot help but ask if bullying had something to do with the shooting.

Many people thought in the beginning that the boys had been victims of bullying, and while this is true, the boys also harassed other students.

Dylan, Eric, and their other friends were known for not only harassing other students but for threatening them and intimidating them. One incident resulted in the other student breaking down into tears are being afraid to go to school.

The boys were known to have a bad temper and to alienate students with his behavior.

However, Eric and Dylan both made comments in their journals about getting back at those that had mistreated them or left them out. However, when we look at the people who were shot, it was not just people who had bullied the boys but it was everyone.

While if the boys had been bullied, it seems that they would have focused their attack on those that had bullied them, bombs were placed out in the parking lot so that they would kill rescue workers, parents, law enforcement, as well as the media.

The attack was not focused on a group of people who bullied the two boys, but instead, it showed that both boys just wanted to kill people. Eric wrote in his journal that he wanted to be remembered for committing the deadliest attack in the history of the US. He stated that he wanted to leave a lasting impression on the entire world.

While the harassment that the boys were experiencing at school may have given them an excuse to go on a rampage, there was much more going on inside of their minds than being angry doing to mistreatment.

Eric Harris once wrote that he wanted to be godlike, to be the judge of who dies and who lives, on the 20th of April in 1999 he made that wish come true.

Today, there are mental health professionals that believe that we can tell if someone as young as 3 is at risk for becoming a psychopath, which is a person has the capability of committing crimes such as the Columbine shooting without ever feeling a bit of guilt or remorse for their actions.

There are also mental health professionals that believe Eric Harris was showing signs of what they call a budding psychopath.

According to Dr. Frank Ochberg who is a psychiatry professor at Michigan State University, and who took part in the FBI school-shooting symposium, which was held not long after the Columbine shootings, the two boys most likely would not have taken part in the shooting if they had to do it without the other boy. He dubbed them as a deadly duo.

Dylan, according to Ochberg was a hot head and suffered from depression, however, Eric was cool and calculated. It was Eric who did not react to discipline and had always found it easy to read others.

Ochberg stated that he believed that Eric was on his way to becoming a psychopath because he had almost no conscience.

The lack of a conscience is the trademark of someone that is a psychopath, which only makes up 1 percent of the entire population.

Many believed that Eric suffered from psychosis where he would be out of touch with reality or would experience delusions or hallucinated, however, it is believed that Eric knew exactly what he was doing which would categorize him as a psychopath.

A psychopath does not comprehend that their actions are going to hurt people, they lack any empathy or remorse.

Both Dylan and Eric lived their lives in quiet desperation which was fueled by each other's hatred. Both of these boys suffered from mental illness and believed that they suffered from some type of rejection.

Many people wanted to blame the Columbine shooting on video games because according to news reports as well as the boys' journals, they loved to play violent games for hours on end.

We asked ourselves if because the boys had been exposed to the violence in the video games, they had been desensitized to what guns could actually do.

According to a report that was published by the BBC, on May 1, 2001, the families of those that had been killed in the shooting were seeking damages from the game makers claiming that the games played a role in the shooting.

The lawsuit claimed that the games that were produced by 25 different companies were what created the conditions which made the shooting possible.

Some claimed that because when a person is playing a video game such as Doom, there is no detachment from the character you are playing.

In fact, some mental health professionals stated that when you are playing this specific game as well as games like it, you are not controlling the character but instead, you are the character in the game.

However, it is these same mental health professionals that will tell you that the boys felt no guilt for destroying the lives of their peers and teachers, which is a classic sign of a psychopath.

While we will probably never know just how much video games influenced the boys it is safe to say that because they were already suffering from mental illnesses, they could have been influenced, however, that does not mean that the video games were completely to blame for the shooting.

Finally, many people started asking about the Goth subculture that it was rumored the boys were part of, however, this was nothing more than a theory.

There is one thing that all of these theories have in common and that is that they make the boys, Eric Harris and Dylan Klebold the victims in the situation.

Looking back, it is astonishing to see how so many tried to hold on to the idea that these two teenage boys were the victims in the attack instead of the perpetrators.

Now we understand that the boys wanted to commit murder. They wanted to see people die. Simply thumbing through their journals will tell you that much.

While these boys did suffer from mental illness, they were being treated, they had good families, and strong support systems in place. We may never truly understand the reasoning behind the shooting, but one thing is for sure. There were 12 students and 1 teacher that were the victims of this massacre, Dylan Klebold, and Eric Harris, they were the perpetrators and their intention was to kill.

Eric Harris's Childhood

On the 9th of April, 1981 Eric Harris was born in Wichita, Kansas. Eric's father was an Air Force pilot, which meant that Eric moved around quite a bit when he was a child.

When the family lived in Plattsburg, New York, Eric seemed just like any other kid. However, after his father retired and the family moved in 1993 to Littleton, Colorado, Eric began to slowly change.

Eric played soccer and wore preppy clothes, but still struggled to fit in. It was when he entered high school that he and Dylan Klebold, who was also a social outcast, became friends.

Klebold as a shy boy but Harris was volatile and very talkative. The two hated the school as well as the jocks, and everyone that they though mistreated them. It was this bond that created the environment that would lead to the shootings.

Both of the boys became captivated by Hitler as well as the Nazis while they were studying German, even wearing swastikas.

Eric's anger was usually very easy to see. Once when angry at a friend, Eric threw a ball of ice at the boy's windshield and cracked the glass. Later, Eric made a threat against the boy's life on his website.

Eric often posted on his website about the people that he thought had been mean to him or who had mistreated him, going off on violent rants.

Both Eric and Dylan were arrested in 1998 when, after stealing items from a van which they had broken into. Both boys were then charged with criminal trespassing, theft, and criminal mischief. Because this was the boy's first offense, both of them were enrolled in a program which required them to take part in counseling as well as community service.

The boys were released from the program in 1999 just two months before the massacre.

The boys' reports that were given at when the program ended, which stated that Eric was a very bright and his chances of succeeding in life were high.

Eric made good grades while he was in school, however, most of his work contained gory details or violent imagery.

After Eric was arrested for breaking into the van, he and Dylan began planning their attack on their school. The boys referred to it as "Judgement Day," and wanted to kill hundreds. They hoped that they would become somewhat famous while they were taking their revenge on those that they believed had done them wrong.

The two learned how to get their hands on guns and how to make bombs. Several videotapes were also recorded where the boys discussed their plan. The tapes were filled with pure hatred, racist remarks, as well as the boys showing some concern for what their parents would go through.

Just before the shooting Eric was rejected by the US Marine Corps, due to the Luvox that he was taking for depression, many people wonder if this did not add fuel to the already existing fire.

Dylan Klebold's Childhood

Born in Lakewood, Colorado on September 11, 1981, no one ever suspected that Dylan Klebold would kill 13 people.

His father was a geophysicist and his mother worked with people who were disabled, then the couple started their own company in real estate management. Dylan grew up living an upper-middle-class lifestyle and was a very intelligent boy.

In elementary, Dylan had been placed in a program that was for the gifted students and was often described as shy. Growing up, Dylan was an all-American boy who loved the Boston Red Sox and enjoyed playing baseball.

In ninth grade, he became friends with Eric Harris as well as Brooks Brown. Dylan was like most teenagers, he enjoyed playing violent video games, like to bowl, and he worked as the sound man for school productions. Dylan also worked with Eric at the local pizza place for a little while.

Dylan took an interest in technology which meant that he did not fit in with the rest of the kids at Columbine because the school had a very strong jock culture and began to develop hatred toward the school and his peers.

This is one thing that he had in common with Eric Harris. The two together created what they called The Trench Coat Mafia, which was a clique for the social outcasts.

The group was known for wearing dark colored clothes, and long coats.

While it was known that Dylan was very bright, he earned mediocre grades in school because he did not apply himself.

Dylan was charged with Eric for breaking into the van and stealing items out of it. Both were given the same punishment.

In the writings that were found after the shooting, it was found that Dylan was very depressed because he did not have a relationship with a girl and he expressed thoughts of suicide.

The writings were full of rage as were the essays and poems that he had written for his English class and his creative writing class. All of the writings were filled with images of war, death, and blood.

One sign that was overlooked that things were dire for both boys was a video that they two made for a school project where they depicted themselves as heroes who shot all of the jocks in the hallways of the school.

In one video that Dylan and Eric made before the shooting, Dylan stated that he hoped he and Eric were able to kill 250 of his classmates and compared the shooting to Doom, the boys' favorite video game.

In the same video, the boys talked about who should direct the movie made about the attack.

The Warning Signs

After the Columbine shooting, many people wondered if there had been any warning signs that something of that magnitude would occur and many believe that there were definite signs that were overlooked.

According to Ken Salazar, who was the Attorney General in Colorado at the time, Eric had 15 run-ins with the law before the shooting occurred.

While some of the incidents were not serious such as when he got in trouble for throwing snowballs, there were other more serious incidents such as when he broke into the van or when the threatened to kill his neighbor.

The threats had been found in a notebook that was located at the Sheriff's Department after the shooting, however, at the time the threats were reported, a report was filed but nothing was ever done.

It also seemed that those who were in charge of security knew Columbine was the kind of place that a shooting could occur. Howard Cornell and Joe Schallmoser who were in charge of security had just eight months before the attack written a plan which ensured that anyone working at the school report not only to parents but to law enforcement if they heard about any threats of violence that students were making.

It is reported that those who worked at Columbine did not follow the plan. At the time that the plan was presented to the school, officials were already aware that Harris could be a danger.

They were informed that both boys were collecting weapons and that they boys were posting their plans on Eric's website.

Brooks Brown was a junior in 1998 at Columbine and in March of that year, he found that Eric had posted his name on his website, along with death threats.

Brooks stated that he was stunned by what he saw no the page; Eric had posted that he wanted not just to beat the boy up but that he wanted to blow him up. Eric also stated on the website that he was making pipe bombs which he would use to do it.

Judy and Randy Brown, Brooks' parents also stated that they were horrified by what was posted on the website and afraid of Eric.

The two took the pages from Eric's website to the Sheriff's Office and were told that Eric had a criminal file. They were informed that both Eric and Dylan were on probation after breaking into a vehicle and stealing the contents.

The family was dumbfounded when the Sheriff did nothing about the treats. The Sheriff's department later denied that anyone had ever spoken in person with any of the Brown's.

However, after the paperwork was uncovered by CBS News, which showed that a warrant had been obtained for Eric's home and a pipe bomb had been found which was consistent with the pipe bombs that Eric had written about on his website. Yet, Eric's house was never searched. The Sheriff's department had not even sent one officer to the house.

The Browns notified the Sheriff's Department of what was on the website in April 1998 which was one entire year before the shootings occurred.

After the Sheriff met with the Brown family, they did contact school administrators and inform them that it was possible that Eric was making the bombs. Sally Blanchard, from the school's district office, stated that there was no reason for the school to look into the matter.

She later stated that the school officials had been informed by the Sheriff's Department that there was an investigation going on and that the school did not need to take action. She stated that no action was taken because the school did not want to interfere with the investigation.

No one from the school spoke to Eric's teachers, friends or even his family about him or the treats.

One of Eric's friends, Nate Dykeman stated that both Eric and Dylan had shown their weapons to several people before the shooting took place.

Devon Adams found her name on Eric's hit list that was located on his website when she was a sophomore in 1998 at Columbine.

Devon told the assistant principal, however, the assistant principal denies that the conversation ever took place. By the time Devon, found her name on the list, the two boys had two sawed-off shotguns, a rifle, and a semi-automatic pistol.

The boys reportedly made videos of themselves as they shot the guns and often played the videos in the school, however, the school would not comment stating that they could not disclose if any of the teachers had seen the tapes.

According to Blanchard, what people did see was that both boys went to class every day, they turned their assignments in, both were trying to improve their grades, both boys had friends and both of the boys were making plans for the future.

In February, just a few months before the shooting Dylan wrote a story about a person who wore a black trench coat shooting students and then bombing the city. He even stated that he understood the actions of the assassin in the story.

His teacher stated that it was "the most vicious story I've ever read." After reading the story she spoke to both Dylan's parents and the school counselor, but nothing was ever done.

This was another missed opportunity where had action been taken quickly, it may have stopped the shooting.

According to the school officials, the plan that Cornell and Schallmoser had written up only applied if an employee of the school became aware of any student who had threatened to kill someone which according to them, did not apply when it came to Eric and Dylan.

However, the plan actually stated that any threat toward another student or a threat of committing an act of violence. Which did apply when it came to Eric.

Many people asked, where the parents were. How could parents, not know that their children were planning on taking guns into a school and shooting their peers? How was it possible that the guns were in the homes, that the boys were making bombs and the parents did not know?

The boys publicly posted on a website that they wanted to kill students, that they wanted to blow things up. How could a parent be completely unaware of this?

According to the police, neither of the boy's parents knew that their sons were accumulating an arsenal right under their noses that contained guns, fuses for bombs, more than 100 bombs, gunpowder, and guns.

The boys recorded the videos at night when their parents were asleep and in one of his videos Eric imagined what his parents would say after the shooting was over.

He imagined that they would ask themselves if things would have been different if they had checked his room, or if they had asked him more questions.

Dylan's mother, in an interview with Diane Sawyer, stated that like other parents, she was positive that if there had been something wrong with her son, she would have known about it but that quickly changed after the shooting

His mother was open and honest in her interview, explaining that as parents, we like to think that if something is wrong, we are going to be aware of it. That the love that we have for our children and our understanding will be enough for them.

Sue Klebold however, did not know that something was wrong. She was not able to stop her son from killing people, from harming himself, and she stated that she finds that is very hard to live with.

Sue wanted people to understand that while things may seem perfectly fine, things can be terribly wrong, and the child could be in crisis.

Sue recalled the events of the day stating that she was at work when she received a call from her husband. His voice was shaky and she told him that something bad was happening at the school, that there were two shooters wearing trench coats.

Dylan's father stated that one of Dylan's friends had called concerned that Dylan could have been one of the shooters

Sue's first response as a mother was fear that her child was in danger, but once she arrived home, she found out that it was believed that Dylan was involved.

She said that she remembered thinking that if Dylan was hurting people, he had to be stopped and she prayed that he would die.

Later that day she would find out that her son was, in fact, dead, and that was when she began going back over the time since her son was born, trying to find what signs she had missed.

Sue admitted that her son was filled with hate and cruel, that his behavior was something that she had to own.

Sadly, Sue had no idea that her son was suffering from severe depression until after the shooting. She had noticed that when he reached adolescence, he was not interested in making good grades any longer, that he was spending his time alone in his bedroom and on his computer which he had built.

She stated that he was moody and often irritable, but she believed it was normal teenage behavior.

Sue remembered that there were times when Dylan would be quiet or seem distant. She would ask him if he was okay, but he would tell her that he had a lot of homework or that he was tired and then go to his room.

Sue let Dylan go to his room, however, after the shooting, she stated that she would dig and dig until he gave her some answers.

She was suffering from an illusion that everything was okay, that it would be okay, simply because she loved him so much, a mistake that many parents make.

Sue had no idea that Dylan kept a journal until after the shooting, which was when she began reading them. This led her to realize that her son had been suffering from depression, was very lonely, and suicidal since he was 15 years old.

Reading the journals was very difficult for Dylan's mother because as she was reading them, she wanted to comfort her son, to help him but it was already too late.

Both boys were analyzed by FBI profilers, their writings were looked at as well as the "Basement Tapes," that they had recorded in secret in which their plot to attack the school was discussed.

It was determined that it was very likely that Dylan was suffering from depression and that Eric was a psychopath. Neither of the boys had been diagnosed when they were alive.

According to Dr. Gregory Fritz, of the American Academy of Child and Adolescent Psychiatry, parents naturally tend to ignore as well as rationalize any changes in their children's behavior thinking that it is just a phase.

This can result in the real issue not being recognized. It is believed that up to 20 percent of all high school students have had suicidal thoughts within the last years. It is important for parents to remember that they need to speak to their children if they feel that the child may be experiencing any thoughts of suicide.

According to Dr. Flitz, who has spoken to hundreds of kids that have tried to commit suicide, none of them have stated that it was the fact that someone asked them how they were feeling or spoke to them about suicide that pushed them over the edge.

During Sue's interview with Diane Sawyer, she spoke about a confrontation that she had with Dylan that would a huge regret.

It was about a year and a half before the shooting when Dylan began getting in trouble. He was suspended from school for three days for hacking into the computer system. When another student taunted him at school, he scratched their locker, leaving a nickname to mock the kid.

Of course, after that, we know that the boys were caught breaking into the van and stealing items from inside.

When it was happening, Sue stated that she felt like that was the worst thing that could happen. She also stated that after his arrest, Dylan did not feel as if he had done anything wrong and received a lecture about knowing the difference between right and wrong.

She said she talked to him about the Ten Commandments, that it was wrong to steal and that he had privileges taken away.

There was one night however that she became particularly frustrated at Dylan for not doing his chores which resulted in her pushing him up against the fridge.

She yelled at Dylan to stop being so selfish and had yelled at him that it was Mother's Day and he had completely forgotten.

She said she remembered Dylan softly asking her not to push him, and saying that he did not know how much longer he could control himself.

She thought he was just politely asking her to back off. Afterward, Dylan went and purchased her a Mother's Day gift. Sue thought everything was fine after that.

Dylan had promised that he was going to do better and Sue thought that because Dylan was involved in the juvenile counseling program, things would get better.

It is also important to note that it was at this time that Dylan and Eric began becoming close.

It was this conversation that would be one of the biggest regrets of her life.

When experts look at the Columbine shooting most of them can agree that Eric Harris exhibited behaviors that would signify he was a psychopath.

Eric lacked any conscience and had no empathy, however, he was very charming. He would write in his journals about how he wanted to have guns, about being violent, how he found it easy to lie as well as how he got great pleasure from lying to people.

He would write about his fantasies of getting revenge on people that he believed had insulted him or who had left him out. He also wrote about raping girls.

Dylan other the other hand would draw hearts in his journal and write about finding the love of his life.

Sue spoke about Eric, stating that he had been very polite. She had met Eric's parents, stating that her children were not allowed to play with anyone until they met the kid's parents and went to their home.

According to Sue, Eric's parents were very kind and seemed to be responsible adults.

It was another mother that warned Sue about Eric's anger, however, Sue didn't believe the mother because Eric had been so polite when he was around her.

She did state that she did not blame Eric's parents for what he had done, that she still speaks to them occasionally and that they are not Eric, nor should his behavior represent them.

When asked about the Trench Coat Mafia, she stated that she had heard the phrase, but that it seemed more like a group of kids that like to wear the same type of coat, not a real organized group.

She also stated that when Dylan was accepted to college, she had quit checking his room, deciding that it was time to give him privacy. However, had she continued checking, she may have found the weapons hidden in the room and may have been able to take the steps to stop the shooting.

While she did state that if she had checked his room, she would have been violating his privacy which would have damaged their relationship and that she would have rather that he had shared her thoughts with her, had she the chance to do it over, she would have checked his room every day as if his life depended on it.

Dr. Mary Ellen O'Toole, a former FBI agent, stated that parents need to understand that they do have the right to check their children's bedrooms.

If there is a room in your home, that you are paying the mortgage on, which you are not allowed in, there is a serious problem, according to Dr. O'Toole.

Of course, it does not mean that the child is going to go out and murder people, but it does mean that the child is hiding something and it is your job as the parent to find out what is going on.

Dylan had at one point, during his senior year, asked her to purchase him a gun. He was told no because guns were not kept in their home, however, he was able to get the girl that he took to the senior prom to purchase three for him, legally.

Dylan told the girl that the guns were going to be used when he went hunting. Sue stated that before the shooting, she did not even know that the two boys had gone to the shooting range to practice.

Dylan's mother believes that if she had recognized the warning signs, she could have stopped Dylan from participating in the shooting.

It was only two months before the shooting when Dylan's English teacher met with Sue to discuss a story that Dylan had written. In the story, a man that wore a black trench coat had a duffle bag full of weapons, and shot all of the students that he called the 'college preps.'

Sue and her husband asked Dylan about the paper on two different occasions, however, after being told that he did not have it both times, they dropped the topic, not understanding just how serious the situation was.

The counselor of the high school stated that at the time he had not seen the writing as a threat.

While one single writing that he had done for his class may not have been such a huge deal or a reason to take action, however, added to all of the other pieces of the puzzle, it would have been a reason for concern.

Violent writings are not enough to cause someone to jump to the conclusion that someone is going to commit a violent crime, however, it should be a red flag.

The violent writings of young people need to be looked at and the person evaluated.

Sue believes that if she had recognized that something was going on with her son, she could have prevented him from being one of the shooters.

In her book, *A Mother's Reckoning, Living in the Aftermath of Tragedy,* Sue Klebold wrote, "Like mothers all over Littleton, I had been praying for my son's safety. But when I heard the newscaster pronounce twenty-five people dead, my prayers changed. If Dylan was involved in hurting or killing other people, he had to be stopped. As a mother, this was the most difficult prayer, I had ever spoken in the silence of my thoughts, but in that instant, I knew the greatest mercy, I could pray for was not my son's safety, but for his death."

April 20, 1999

Dylan Klebold was supposed to be meeting his bowling club that morning. Normally he was hard to wake up, but on the morning of April 20th, Dylan bounced down the stairs before his mother had even finished dressing.

She called out to him, "Bye," was his only reply as the front door closed heavily behind him. There was something strange about his voice that morning, but his father promised Sue Klebold that he would talk to Dylan as soon as he got home from school that evening.

That morning at 9 AM as the morning announcements were scrolling across the television screen at Columbine High School, one message read, "Today is not a good day to be here."

At 11:10 that morning, the boys arrived at the school in separate vehicles. The carried CO_2 bombs, a 9mm handgun, 2 sawed-off shotguns, a semi-automatic handgun, and duffle bags which contained 2 20-pound propane bombs.

The bombs had been programmed to go off at 11:17 AM. The explosives were large enough that had they gone off they could have easily killed 500 people.

Brooks Brown, who had severed his relationship with Eric the year before, after Eric had thrown a chunk of ice through his windshield was standing outside the school on the morning of the shooting.

He and Eric had just patched their relationship up and he was surprised to find that Eric was just showing up to school after 11 am. Eric was usually very serious about his work and about being on time.

Brooks teasingly scolded Eric. Eric told Brooks that it didn't matter anymore then stated that he liked Brooks now. He told Brooks to get out of there and to go home.

Brooks did just as he was told, and left the school grounds very quickly.

After the boys placed the duffel bags in the cafeteria, they returned to their cars to wait for their bombs to go off. They had planned on shooting anyone that ran out of the school.

The bombs, however, did not explode and at 11:19 AM, the police received a 911 call from Brooks, who had borrowed a cell phone, informing them that there had been shots fired at the school.

At the same time, another call was received stating that there had been an explosion just 3 miles southwest of the school. The caller stated that Eric and Dylan were standing on the west steps of the school and were wearing black trench coats.

11:19 AM Eric Harris and Dylan Klebold open fire on the students that are sitting outside of the west entrance of the school, killing two and injuring five.

Some of the students as well as the teachers who had witnessed the shooting believed it to be nothing more than a senior prank and thought nothing of it.

11:20 Dylan leans into the cafeteria, but then rejoins Eric on the stairs. Eric shoots Anne Marie Hochhalter several times as she tries to get to the cafeteria.

While the boys are outside, witnesses see them tossing lit bombs onto the roof of the school. Several staff members ran into the school yelling for the students to get under the cafeteria tables.

Deputy Gardner pulled up to the school's west entrance.

11:30 Many of the students had escaped the building using the east entrance. They hid behind a police car and informed the officer that the boys were inside, randomly shooting people and throwing grenades.

Dylan and Eric are located in the library. In only 7.5 minutes they kill 10 and leave 12 more wounded. There were 56 people in the library at the time, 34 were left unharmed.

More officers arrive on the scene and it is reported that gun shots from a large caliber rifle have been heard. Smoke is reported as coming out of the school.

Realizing how dangerous the situation is, one of the officers calls the Sheriff's office to request help.

11:35 The last victim of the shooting is killed. The boys walk the halls, looking into the windows of some of the classrooms to which the doors are locked. The students reported that they did not try to break in or harm them, but that they only made eye contact.

It is at this time that more bombs are thrown into the cafeteria. The security camera shows one of them exploding.

11:40 AM It is reported that 30 students have escaped from the school and are hiding behind police cars. It is reported that these students had escaped from the library after Dylan and Eric headed for the science wing.

It is believed that one of the boys has left the school and police begin to surround the school.

The school surveillance system records the boys shooting at the duffle bags that they had placed in the cafeteria. The bombs do not explode.

11:50- Eric and Dylan are in the school office area. One officer reports that shots were fired near the east end of the school.

The sprinkler system in the cafeteria is activated. A bomb is reported at the intersection of Wadsworth and Chatfield.

Officers report hearing shots near the northeast section of the school. The boys seem to be moving through the school randomly.

12:00 Both boys leave the cafeteria, then go to the library which is located upstairs. A request for an armored vehicle is made because it was unsafe for any medical vehicles to be in the area to help the wounded.

Officers begin reporting that students are slowly evacuating the building. They see the boys in the window of the library and shoot at them. The boys shoot back at the police.

The SWAT team arrived.

12:02 The boys arrive at the library and walk to a window opening fire on the police. At this time, there were 12 dead students and one teacher that was dying as well as 24 staff and students that had been injured.

Just 6 minutes after walking into the library, the boys walked to a bookshelf. In unison, they counted to three and shot themselves. Eric had placed his shotgun in his mouth and shot himself in the roof of his mouth. Dylan shot himself in the left side of the head using a semi-automatic handgun.

The victims were:

Dave Sanders- A teacher. The third to be shot and the last to die.

Racheal Scott

Daniel Rohrbough

Kyle Velasquez

Steven Curnow

Cassie Bernall

Isaiah Shoels

Matthew Kechter

Lauren Townsend

John Tomlin

Kelly Fleming

Daniel Mauser

Corey Depooter

On April 21st, a 20-pound propane tank bomb, that Dylan and Eric had planted, is found in the school's kitchen. According to reports, had the bomb gone off, hundreds more would have been killed.

On April 26th, the police learn that Dylan's girlfriend had purchased three of the guns that had been used in the shooting and given them to Dylan just a few days after she turned 18.

May 3rd, Mark E Manes age 22 faces felony charges for selling a minor a handgun. He admits that he did sell the handgun to the boys for 500 dollars, however, denies that he knew anything about their plans. The students of Columbine return to school at Chatfield High.

May 20th, on the one-month anniversary of the Columbine shootings, a 15-year-old walks into a school carrying two handguns and shoots his classmates in Conyers, Georgia. Six students were injured; no one was killed.

May 22nd, the seniors of Columbine High graduate. A moment of silence is held for those that had been killed in the shooting.

June 1st, the students of Columbine return to the school to collect their belongings.

June 3rd, work begins on the school so the students can return to class in August.

June 16th, it is announced that according to the video surveillance of the shooting, there was no third shooter, even though it had been rumored that there was.

June 17th Philip Joseph Duran is charged with providing a handgun to minors, for introducing Eric and Dylan to Mark Manes.

September 24th, Howard Cornell retires after a disagreement on how the school can best protect the students in the future.

October 12th, CBS obtained a copy of a portion of the surveillance videos from the cafeteria of the shooting and aired it. The tape had been released to law enforcement agencies to help them better understand how to deal with school shootings.

October 19th, a 17-year-old student from Columbine is arrested for stating that he was going to finish what Eric and Dylan had started.

October 25th, Eric's parents Kath and Wayne Harris finally agree to meet with the investigators for the first time, and only if specific questions were not asked, such as whether Eric's father had found one of the pipe bombs his son had made and set it off in a field with Eric.

November 2nd, Brenda Parker, who was Eric Harris's former girlfriend claimed that Arthur Thomas had sent her a threat via the internet.

November 12th, Mark Manes receives a six-year sentence for selling the handgun to the boys.

The Aftermath

It was April 20th, 1999 that would change the schools in America forever. School violence has been documented through the history of the US, however, it was the Columbine shooting that caused a shift to occur in the schools.

The shooting was covered extensively by the media which caused fear to sweep over the nation and chaos followed.

Many people started to believe that the schools were no longer a safe place for their children and they felt that something had to be done to prevent any more attacks on the schools.

It was the Columbine shooting, which created the conditions which are still felt today in public schools. Parents, students, and teachers fear that the schools are not safe.

Because of the attack at Columbine, zero-tolerance policies were put into place in all of the schools across the United States and student profiling intensified.

The Columbine shooting was not the first shooting to take place in a school in the US, however, none of the other shootings caused as much chaos as the Columbine shooting did. Mostly because the media did not cover those shootings like they did the one at Columbine.

There were a string of shootings beginning in 1997 however, they did not affect school policy. The public knew about the shootings, they were afraid that schools were becoming more violent, however, when not a single school shooting occurred from 1998 until Columbine, the fear began to fade.

The country was at this time focusing on other issues besides school violence. It was during that time that the Department of Education did a survey and found that before the Columbine attacks, less than 5 percent of all US students feared that they would be attacked while at school.

After the attack at Columbine, most Americans began to fear that schools were not safe. This occurred mainly because of the amount of coverage that the shooting got. Before Columbine, no school shooting had been televised.

What made Columbine different is that people gathered around their televisions and watched the murders occur. This created an intense sense of fear and changed the way that Americans thought about schools.

While we know that the events that occurred at Columbine alone were enough to cause public panic and fear, the media coverage made things far worse.

It was only 28 minutes after the attack had occurred that the new stations began going on the air covering the shooting, with stories that were incorrect. They gave the public the wrong information and caused confusion.

Even though the first reports were inaccurate, the story still sparked fear in the public. The interviewed students that had been in the building, showed video of the kids running out of the school, their hands in the air and tears streaming down their faces.

It was these initial reports that caused the media to pay so much attention to the shooting then and in the years that followed.

In the first 10 days after the attack, 43 broadcasts were made about it. Even a week after the shooting USA Today still had 10 separate stories about the Columbine shooting in one paper.

It was two weeks after the shooting before the New York Times stopped mentioning the Columbine shooting on the front page.

The coverage that the Columbine shooting received was record-breaking and Americans were constantly forced to face the events that had taken place.

The media made it clear that a shooting just like the one that had happened in Columbine could happen in any school in the United States. However, according to studies that were done at the time, the school was one of the safest places that children could be.

In the months that followed, the media began looking for more information that would keep the viewer's attention, releasing the home videos that Dylan and Eric had made, providing information about the shooters, and even releasing images from the inside of the school during the shooting.

This continued to cause more fear as people had to send their children to school every day while still facing all of this media coverage, and wondering if their child's school would be next.

Within one week of the Columbine shooting, a copycat threat had been made in each of the 49 mainland states. It was reported that in Pennsylvania alone, over 60 threats had been made.

Just one month after the shooting over 350 students across the nation had been arrested for making threats against their schools.

Many of the threats that were made were made by kids who had no intention of committing any actual violence, however, there was no way to determine which threats were real and which were fake.

There were copycat attacks, though. In 2007 Seung-Hui Cho, a student at Virginia Tech walked onto campus, killed 32 people, and injured 17 more.

In the middle of the attack, Cho mailed letters as well as videos to NBC in which he stated that he wanted to be a martyr like Dylan and Eric of Columbine.

More threats were made after this using Columbine as a reference and the fear of more school violence became a part of the American culture.

After the shooting at Columbine, the way parents thought about schools shifted. Just one year after the shooting, a study showed that 71 percent of parents whose children attended school felt that the events that had occurred at Columbine had changed the way they felt when it came to their child's safety at school.

Less than 40 percent of the parents that were surveyed felt that their children were safe at school.

The way that students felt about school changed as well. 1/3 of all students surveyed stated that they believed there was someone who attended their school who was capable of the violence that was seen at Columbine.

Children had to go to school every day, knowing that what had happened at Columbine could happen to them as well.

Because both parents and students feared that the schools were no longer safe, the way school violence was handled changed.

Before the Columbine shooting, it was believed that school violence only happened in certain areas, mainly in the urban areas.

Columbine, however, was located in a suburban area which seemed to shake people to their core. Realizing that school violence could occur at any school, in any neighborhood caused the citizens to demand the schools reform their security policies.

This "Columbine-Effect, led to widespread changes as well as new policies in schools across the nation.

After the Columbine shooting, American schools created new policies that would help to prevent another event like it from occurring.

Zero tolerance policies spread quickly across the nation, ensuring that action was taken quickly whenever a student threatened another, possessed drugs, or any type of weapon on school grounds. The punishment was usually expulsion or suspension.

Millions of dollars were spent by schools, installing metal detectors and hiring extra security guards. Some small towns hired extra police officers that would work specifically in the schools during their shifts.

While all of this made parents and students feel better about the safety of the schools, there is little evidence that it stopped any attacks from occurring. Today, all of these policies, metal detectors, and other extra security measures are a reminder of that terrible day when Eric Harris and Dylan Klebold walked into their school and killed 13 people.

After the shooting, people began to fear that there could be students in their schools just like Eric and Dylan.

It seemed that every school had one student that was making a 'to kill' list. One day they would be sitting next to you in class, the next they were gone, and you would find yourself wondering if you were on that list. Had you done anything to that person to make them hate you enough to want to kill you?

Our schools were no longer a place where we could go to learn as innocent children, but now they were a place where we had to wonder if someone was going to kill us.

For some, it was a reality. According to the data that was compiled, there were 14 cases of attempted copycat shootings on the anniversary of the Columbine shooting.

The people involved in 13 of those cases claimed that their intention was to kill more people than Eric and Dylan had.

In 10 of the case, those who were involved thought of Eric and Dylan as gods, martyrs, idols, or heroes.

Three of the cases involved students who had visited Columbine. Two of those that had visited Columbine attacked their schools, and one of them was stopped.

There has been a total of 74 known copycat cases. 21 of those were attacks, while the other 53 were pots or threats that got the attention of law enforcement.

Out of those who plotted to or did attack their schools, 95 percent were males. There were only 4 females that had made threats and none of the threats ended in an attack.

The average age of the attackers was 17. 53 percent of all of the cases involved guns while 18 percent of the plotters or attackers used bombs, and only 14 percent involved knives.

Out of the known copycat cases, 89 lives were lost, 126 students were killed, and 9 of the shooters committed suicide.

On November 19th, 1999 Victor Cordova Jr., who was only 12 years old, shot and killed Aracelia Tena, his 13-year-old classmate. The boy later pleaded guilty to the charges and was sent to juvenile prison for 2 years.

On February 29th, 2000, a 6-year-old boy shot and killed Kayla Rolland, his classmate that was also 6 at the time, while he was at school in Michigan. The boy was not charged with the crime due to his age.

Jamelle James, a 19-year-old who was living with the 6-year-old shooter, was sentenced to two 15-year prison sentences because he had kept his gun in a place that was easily accessible to the boy. The uncle of the boy, who owned the home where the boy lived, was charged with possessing a gun that was stolen, which was used in the shooting.

On May 26th, 2000, 13-year-old Nathaniel Brazill, who was an honor student, walked into school on the last day of class and shot Barry Grunow, his teacher. He was given a 28-year prison sentence.

On March 5th, 2001, a 15-year-old boy named Charles Williams walked into a school in Santee California and opened fire. He killed two and injured 13. Williams was given a 50-years to life sentence.

On September 24th, 2003, a 15-year-old boy named John Jason McLaughlin from Minnesota, shot and killed two classmates named Arron Rollins who was 17 and Seth Bartell who was 15. McLaughlin was convicted and given a life sentence.

On March 21st, 2005 Jeff Weise a 16-year-old boy killed his grandfather as well as his grandfather's companion before heading to his school and killing five students, a security guard, as well as a teacher, then he killed himself.

On November 8th, 2005, a 15-year-old boy by the name of Kenneth Bartley walked into his school in Jacksboro, Tennessee, and killed Ken Bruce who was the assistant principal then wounded two other faculty members. He was charged with reckless homicide, which he was found guilty of, however, he was acquitted of the first-degree murder charge.

On August 30th, 2006, Alvaro Castillo, a 19-year-old former student murdered his father and then opened fire in the parking lot of a North Carolina school. He wounded two. It was reported that he had been obsessed with the Columbine attack.

Police found two pipe bombs as well as two rifles in the van that he had driven to the school. Castillo was found guilty of several charges, including murder. He received a sentence of life without parole.

Before the shooting Castillo had sent an email to the principal of Columbine stating that in a few hours, he would hear about another school shooting, Castillo stated that he was the one that would be responsible for that shooting. He told the principle that he remembered Columbine and that it was time for the world to remember it. He finished the email with I am sorry.

On the 27th of September 2006, in Bailey, Colorado, an adult gunman entered the school and took six high school girls as hostages. He shot and killed one of them who was 16 at the time, named Emily Keyes. The gunman, Duane Morrison, then took his own life.

On September 29th, 2006, Eric Hainstock, a 15-year-old boy, walked into Weston High School and killed John Klang, the principal at the school. Just the day before, Klang had given Eric a warning because he had been caught with tobacco on school grounds.

On the 2nd of October in 2006, school shootings reached where no one ever suspected they would. A 32-year-old milk-truck driver, named Charles C. Roberts walked into the one-room Amish school located in West Nickel Mines with a gun. He separated all of the female students from the males and then began shooting them. He killed five of the girls, sounded several more and then, killed himself.

On April 16th, 2007, Seung-Hui Cho walked onto the Virginia Tech campus and killed a total of 32 people before he killed himself.

On February 14th, 2008, Steven Kazmierczak, who was 27-years-old, walked into the lecture hall of a university campus located in DeKabl, Illinois, opened fire and killed five students. He injured 18 more and then he shot himself.

The list continues all the way up until today, as I am sure it will continue to do until we find a way to stop the violence at schools across our country.

The Columbine shooting did not just have an effect on the security of our schools, but it also affected student writing.

After the Columbine shooting, people across the nation found themselves asking how they could prevent something like this from occurring again.

The gruesome images that had been aired on every news station was burned into their brains. Once the writings of Eric and Dylan were released, people saw a shocking glimpse of what was going on with the boys.

Dylan had started keeping his journal two years prior to the shootings, entitling it "Existences: A Virtual Book."

He wrote a lot about disappointments that he faced in life, his suicidal thoughts, and love he had lost.

In one of his stories, that he wrote for school, he said, "If I could face an emotion of God, it would have looked like a man. I not only saw his face but also felt emanating from his power, complacence, closure, and godliness. The man smiled and in an instant, though not end or of my own, I understood his actions."

It was in this story that Dylan talked of a tall man in a black trench coat walking onto his college campus and killing the preps.

This story left his teacher confused. She was unsure how to approach it. The teacher spoke with Dylan about the story and he told her that it was only a story. The teacher then contacted the school counselor who was given the same, "it's just a story," line from Dylan.

Teachers gave Eric positive feedback when it came to his extremely violent and graphic writings. It was 1997 when Eric took notice of the school shootings that were in the news. He wrote a paper, stating, "It is just as easy to bring a loaded handgun to school as it is a calculator."

His teacher responded by telling him that the paper was thorough as well as logical. She stated that he had done a nice job.

In 1999, he wrote another paper for the same teacher, which he titled, "Is Murder or Breaking the Law Ever Justified?" It was the same year in which he wrote a paper for a different class where he stated that he was a felon and that spending his nights in jail had changed him.

In the paper, he stated, "I guess it was a worthwhile punishment after all."

The teacher responded with praises, stated that she though the night jail was enough punishment for him. She told him that she was proud of how he had reacted and that it had changed the way he thought. She finished by telling him that she would trust him in a heartbeat.

It was these types of writings that grabbed the attention of investigators after the Columbine shooting, but these types of writings were not unique to Columbine.

When two middle school students from Jonesboro, Arkansas killed four other students as well as a teacher in 1998, there was an article in the newspaper, detailing the regret that his English teacher felt.

The reason that the English teacher was feeling so regretful was that just 14 months before the shooting occurred, one of the boys had turned in a paper to her where he expressed his desire to shoot squirrels. In the paper, he made it clear that the squirrels he was referring to were students and teachers.

After the shooting at Columbine, the school administration had to start paying more attention to the student's writings.

However, it was not only the writings which the students did for school that they were worried about.

One specific event which caused some concern over students losing their first amendment right was when a student was expelled due to content he had written over summer break.

In the content, he talked about raping, sodomizing, a murdering one of his classmates. The writing was taken from his home by another student and later found on the school grounds.

The court claimed that they would be acting irresponsibly, because of the papers that the boys at Columbine and at Jonesboro had written, if they did not take any action against the student that wrote the story.

A separate court held up an expulsion due to the content that a student had posted on his website which he had created at home. The judge said that he appreciated that in the schools, violence was far too common, and due to the Columbine shooting being so fresh in the minds of people all across the country the expulsion would be upheld.

The result was that often students who were given an assignment and stayed within the boundaries provided by their teachers ended up being disciplined for their writing.

One example of this happened in Boston, Massachusetts in 2000. Students were given the assignment to "write a horror story about a mysterious person."

The students had been told that there were no subjects that were off limit when it came to the assignment.

Charles Carithers wrote a horror story about a boy that went into his school with a chainsaw and attacked his English teacher. At the end, it turned out that it was the boy's aunt who had died instead of the English teacher

The teacher reported the boy immediately and he was suspended from school for three days.

Columbine in The Movies

The Columbine shooting inspired many movies which were created by people all across the world. Including:

Bang Bang You're Dead- This movie was originally a play that was inspired not only by the Columbine shooting but Jonesboro as well. In the movie, Trevor Adams, a teenage boy is bullied so badly that he does not think he can handle anymore, but when things look their worst, he gets a second chance when he starts taking part in the Drama Club.

The club decides to put on a play about a murder that happened in a schoolyard, however, the ply risks being shut down due to Trevor's past.

Duck! The Carbine High Massacre- The makers of this film were inspired by the

Columbine shooting and it was one of the first movies that was inspired by Columbine to be released on DVD.

This is not a movie that should be viewed by those that are sensitive nor those who want to see the Columbine shooting take seriously.

Elephant- This film had the highest budget of all of the films that were inspired by Columbine and it is told from the point of view of Brooks, the boy that was let go before the shooting started. This movie was not told by Brooks, nor are any of the events actually true.

Zero Day- This movie is told as if the boys were taping it as they were committing the act of violence against the students of Columbine. It did cause some confusion because there is one particularly graphic scene that looks as if it was shot by a security camera in the library of the school.

In this scene, the boys shoot several students, walk across the tables and eventually shoot themselves, all while you can hear a 911 operator talking on the cell phone of one of the kids that had been shot.

This scene caused a lot of confusion because people believed that these were actual tapes from the shooting. A quick online search for Columbine footage will bring you directly to videos of this scene in the movie.

Many people believed that this was actual footage from the security camera in the Columbine High library, however, if you look at the bottom of the screen you can see the date which is May 1, 2001. Over 2 years after the shooting took place.

Dawn Anna- This is a Lifetime movie was written about the mother of Lauren

Townsend, who was one of the victims of the Columbine shooting. In the movie, Dawn, Lauren's mother, not only survives losing her daughter but a brain tumor as well.

Even though she suffered from many setbacks, Dawn is able to find happiness in her life once again. This movie was made with the permission of Dawn Anna.

April Showers- This movie does not focus on the shooting, or Dylan and Eric but instead, it focuses on the survivors. It shows how those that survived a school shooting moved on with their lives after surviving something so horrific.

Speculation Continues

As I am writing this, it is 18 years after the attack on Columbine, however, the speculation as to why the boys committed the crime still continues.

Those that attended school during that time are now grown and they have children of their own that they send to school every day, even though the events of April 20th, 1999 will forever be burned into their brains.

When they hear that there are police at their child's school, or even just hear sirens go by their home while their children are at school, they cannot help but feel a bit nervous.

Their hearts pound as they fear that history is repeating itself.

At night when they lay their heads down on their pillows, they wonder if they dug deep enough with their own children. They wonder if their children are telling them everything that they need to know about what is going on in their school. They still wonder what exactly caused these boys to attack their school.

There are those that still believe that the boys were taking revenge on those that had bullied them. They believe that the boys had been bullied to the point of wanting to kill hundreds of people and taking their own lives.

There is another group of people who believe that we will never be able to figure out what drove the boys to those horrible acts. We cannot understand what they were going through without being able to speak to them. We don't know what their home lives were truly like. We don't really know what it was like for them at school, from their perspective.

However, according to the FBI, we have to forget the idea that these boys were bullied, we have to forget anything that we have read about the Trench Coat Mafia, and stop thinking that this was for lack of a better word, "simply" a school shooting.

According to the FBI, school shooters are impulsive, they take their rage out on those that have caused them pain whether that be students or faculty.

Eric and Dylan did not act impulsively, but instead, they had planned the shooting for over a year. They wanted to terrorize people all across the nation, not just make those that had upset them pay. These boys had not intended on harming a few people that had upset them, but instead, they wanted to kill hundreds of people.

They were the perfect storm. Hot air met cold air and a tornado was formed. Once that tornado hit the ground, it left damage that no one could have ever imagined in its path.

Knowing that these boys did not attack the school, the students, and the teachers simply because they were bullied can let us rest easier at night and allow us to know that our children are still safe at school.

Today, because of Dylan and Eric, schools are paying more attention to children that could be suffering from mental issues which is what both of these boys were suffering from.

The FBI believes that had it not been for Eric, the shooting would have never happened. This means that we do not have to panic when a child at school is suffering from depression. We do, however, need to help the child find the help and resources that they need.

What we have to watch for is when that hot air meets that cold air and the tornado forms. When the 1 percent of Eric's out there in the world find a boy like Dylan that is hurting inside and only wants to be accepted. That is when things become deadly.

Made in the USA
Lexington, KY
02 November 2018